I0824495

WINTER SPORTS
Maria Koran
EYEDISCOVER

Go to **www.openlightbox.com** and enter this book's unique code.

BOOK CODE

AVD69268

EYEDISCOVER brings you optic readalongs that support active learning.

Published by Lightbox Learning Inc.
276 5th Avenue, Suite 704 #917
New York, NY 10001
Website: www.openlightbox.com

Library of Congress Control Number: 2022935686

ISBN 978-1-7911-4893-5 (hardcover)
ISBN 978-1-7911-4895-9 (multi-user eBook)

Printed in Guangzhou, China
1 2 3 4 5 6 7 8 9 0 26 25 24 23 22

042022
102121

Project Coordinator: John Willis
Designer: Ana María Vidal

Photo Credits
Every reasonable effort has been made to trace ownership and to obtain permission to reprint copyright material. The publisher would be pleased to have any errors or omissions brought to its attention so that they may be corrected in subsequent printings. The publisher acknowledges Alamy, Getty Images, and Shutterstock as its primary image suppliers for this title.

EYEDISCOVER provides enriched content, optimized for tablet use, that supplements and complements this book. EYEDISCOVER books strive to create inspired learning and engage young minds in a total learning experience.

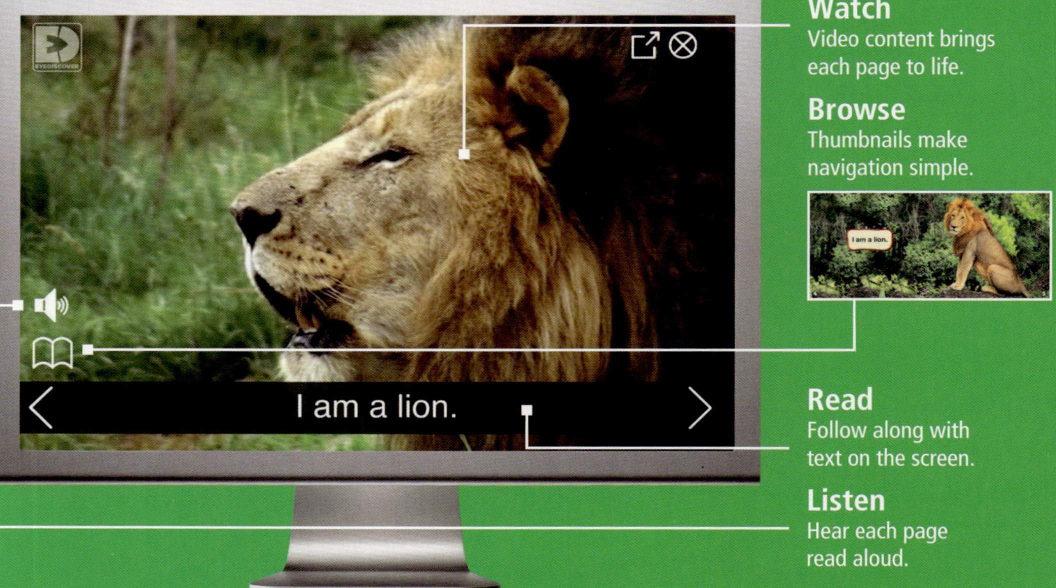

Watch
Video content brings each page to life.

Browse
Thumbnails make navigation simple.

Read
Follow along with text on the screen.

Listen
Hear each page read aloud.

Your EYEDISCOVER Optic Readalongs come alive with...

Audio
Listen to the entire book read aloud.

Video
High resolution videos turn each spread into an optic readalong.

OPTIMIZED FOR

- ☑ TABLETS
- ☑ WHITEBOARDS
- ☑ COMPUTERS
- ☑ AND MUCH MORE!

This title is part of our EyeDiscover digital subscription

1-Year EyeDiscover Subscription
ISBN 978-1-4896-8346-5

Access all EyeDiscover titles with our digital subscription.
Sign up for a FREE trial at **www.openlightbox.com/trial**

In this book, you will learn about

- what they are
- how they are played
- the tools athletes need

and much more!

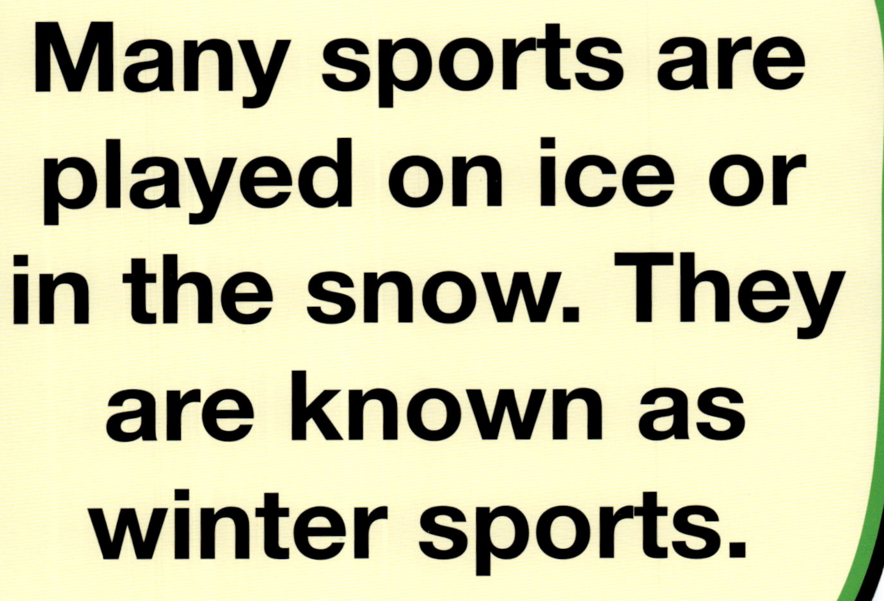

Many sports are played on ice or in the snow. They are known as winter sports.

Hockey is one of the most popular winter sports. Players use sticks to hit a puck into the other team's net.

21

Bobsledding is among the fastest winter sports. Bobsleds can go as fast as a car down an icy track.

USA

USA
BalancePlus
LiteSpeed
BalancePlus

Curlers slide stones on an icy sheet. Players sweep the ice in front of a stone to change how it moves.

BEIJING

Figure skating is both an art and a sport. Skaters do jumps and spins set to music.

There are many skiing sports. Some people ski down hills. Others ski on flat snow. This is called cross-country skiing.

Ski jumpers ski down a ramp and go off a jump at the end. They try to go as far as they can in the air.

modea
20
BWT
BWT
90
91
92
85

Snowboarders go downhill with both feet on one board. Many snowboarding sports have tricks and jumps.

Dog sledding is a sport in which dogs work together to pull a sled. Most racing sled dogs are Alaskan huskies.

WINTER SPORTS BY THE NUMBERS

Bobsleds can go **more than 90 miles per hour** (145 kilometers per hour).

HOCKEY is played in **more than 80 COUNTRIES** around the world.

Curling became a permanent part of the **Winter Olympics** in **1998**.

The longest ski jump was **more than 830 feet** (253 meters).

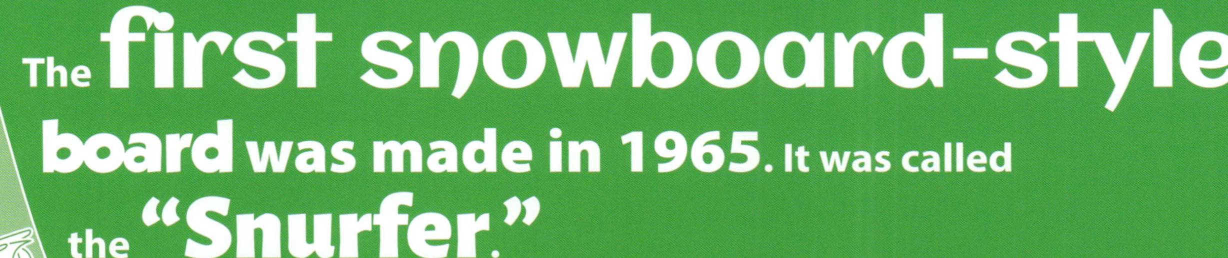

The **first snowboard-style board was made in 1965.** It was called the **"Snurfer."**

A **racing dogsled** may weigh as little as **20 pounds** (9 kilograms).

KEY WORDS

Research has shown that as much as 65 percent of all written material published in English is made up of 300 words. These 300 words cannot be taught using pictures or learned by sounding them out. They must be recognized by sight. This book contains 47 common sight words to help young readers improve their reading fluency and comprehension. This book also teaches young readers several important content words, such as proper nouns. These words are paired with pictures to aid in learning and improve understanding.

Page	Sight Words First Appearance
4	are, as, in, many, on, or, the, they
6	a, into, is, most, of, one, other, to, use
8	an, can, car, down, go
11	change, how, it, moves
13	and, both, do, set
15	country, people, some, there, this
16	air, at, end, far, off, try
19	feet, have, with
20	together, which, work

Page	Content Words First Appearance
4	ice, snow, winter sports
6	hockey, net, players, puck, sticks, team
8	bobsledding, bobsleds, track
11	curlers, sheet, stones
13	art, figure skating, jumps, music, skaters, spins
15	cross-country skiing, hills
16	ramp, ski jumpers
19	board, snowboarders, tricks
20	Alaskan huskies, dogs, dog sledding, sled

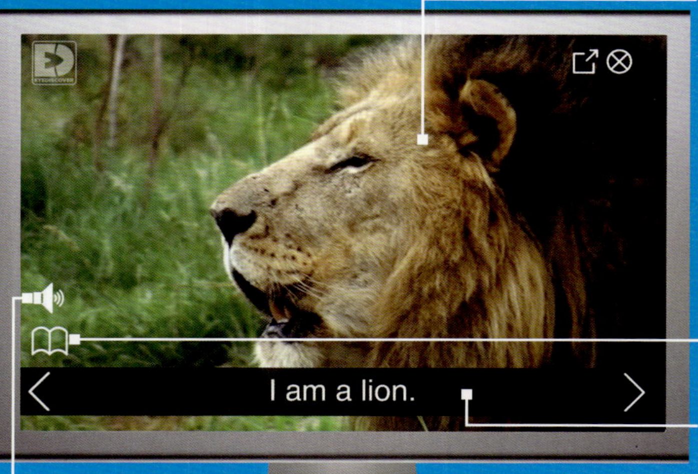

Watch
Video content brings each page to life.

Browse
Thumbnails make navigation simple.

Read
Follow along with text on the screen.

Listen
Hear each page read aloud.

Go to www.openlightbox.com and enter this book's unique code.

BOOK CODE

AVD69268